THE SLEEPY LITTLE BEAR

WRITTEN BY COURTNEY LANDIN
ILLUSTRATED BY YANDEH SALLAH

Author: Courtney Landin
Graphic Design: Katarina Lapidoth
Illustrations: Yandeh Sallah
Editing: Maria Viklund and Lisa Ferland

The Sleepy Little Bear/Courtney Landin
ISBN 978-91-519-8213-7
First Edition

Note to the parents:

This story is written to help your child learn how to relax their body and get ready to fall asleep. It's important that your child can learn how to relax and fall asleep without needing extra help because this allows them to fall back to sleep if they wake up at night. It is normal for a child to wake at night and it's healthy for them to know to fall back to sleep when this occurs. Before you begin using this story, read the section in the back pages of the book called *Happy Sleep Tips* and learn how to set your child up for sleep success.

Read this story in a slow, quiet, and calm way to promote sleep. You might feel silly at first reading like you are talking to them in this type of a voice, but this promotes a relaxation response in the body. Talk quietly and slowly, while stopping to take deep breaths throughout the book. If you choose, after a day or two once you know the story, you can turn off the lights and tell the story to your child, and let them relax while they listen. 

You'll see in the book, "pause, deep breath in and out." This is where you will pause and take a breath in and out. You can either ask your child to do it with you or you can do it on your own. If you do it on your own, notice if your child also does it!

Whether reading the book or reciting it, begin by saying, "Now it's time to get ready for sleep. Take a deep, calming breath in, and breathe out slowly. Feel your body becoming heavy and relaxed in your bed. Let's read about the sleepy little bear."

Let's pretend you are a little bear walking in the
forest. You see a beautiful blue, calm lake. The lake
is very still and not moving at all. There's a green
forest around the lake, and the orange sun is setting,
which means it is sleepy time. You can see some
of the other animals in the forest are also getting
ready for bed.

The papa bunny is
putting his baby
bunnies to sleep
in their tree hollow.
Their fuzzy bunny
bodies are curled
up cozy and tight.

You see the mama bird putting her baby birds to sleep in
their nest. They tuck their tiny beaks into their feathers
and close their eyes.

The fox mama and papa are putting their baby kits to sleep.
Their long tails wrap around, and they cozy down in their
warm, dark den.

Everyone you walk past is settling down for the night.

(pause, deep breath in and out)

You and your mama and papa are walking through the woods and on your way home.

You are so sleepy after a long day of playing in the forest. All day long you climbed up rocks and grassy hills. But now, it is no longer play time. It is time for sleep.

(pause, deep breath in and out)

Together, you slowly walk toward your cozy
cave that is warm and dark. As you crawl inside,
it is time to get ready for bed.

(pause, deep breath in and out)

You brush your bear teeth and make sure they are nice and clean. Now, you are ready to relax.

You crawl into your little bed, and you wrap up tight in a warm blanket as you settle down to sleep. Mama and Papa bear give you a kiss goodnight and leave the room.

(pause, deep breath in and out)

You feel so warm and cozy in your
dark cave, and your eyes feel so heavy.

Clear your mind. Think about the calm, clear lake
you passed earlier. Notice how still the surface is.
Imagine your mind is like the lake. Calm and still.

(pause, deep breath in and out)

Your bed is so soft, and your body relaxes as you close your sleepy eyes. Your furry head feels heavy resting on your soft pillow, and you feel safe and warm. Now think of all the little animals that you saw going to sleep. They were all so cozy and relaxed in their beds.

Take a deep breath in and breathe out slowly. Notice how heavy your body feels as it sinks deeper into your bed. You relax your baby bear legs. Your legs feel heavy and sink further into your bed.

(pause, deep breath in and out)

Your big baby bear belly goes up and down as you breathe
in and out so deeply. So slowly.

(pause, deep breath in and out)

You feel safe and warm in your bed. Tomorrow you will
be ready for a new day after a long sleep tonight.

Your body continues to feel heavy and relaxed in your
bed. It is time to sleep now, my sleepy little bear. Your
heavy body is drifting off to sleep.

(pause, deep breath in and out)

Goodnight, goodnight, my sleepy little bear.

Happy Sleep Tips

Falling asleep is more than just reading a story to your child. You must help prepare their body for sleep so that the combination of a bedtime routine, room environment, and a relaxing story helps them fall asleep and stay asleep.

Setting up for sleep

A consistent routine is an important cue for your child's body to help them know that sleep is coming soon. It helps to prepare the body and mind for sleep. Be sure to limit the amount of time your child spends on a screen before bedtime and set up a consistent bedtime routine.

Eliminate screen time

Screens include televisions, phones, tablets, and e-readers! If watching a screen is part of your child's bedtime routine, adjust the time when they are allowed to watch a show, and then replace the time at bedtime with a book! Any type of blue-light will delay the release or production of melatonin (the sleep hormone) and make it that much harder to sleep. A minimum of one hour without any screens is best before bedtime.

Setting up the room environment

Make sure your child's room is set up for sleep. We sleep best when the room is:

DARK – so dark, in fact, that you can't see your own hand in front of your face! Use blackout curtains or double up your curtains to block out any light from outside. If this isn't possible, make the room as dark as you can.

COOL – 16 to 20 degrees Celsius / 65 to 72 degrees Fahrenheit or cooler depending on the season. Our body temperature drops before falling asleep and this helps set the stage for our bodies.

QUIET – a quiet room is the best sleep environment. White noise is a great way to have the room quiet. White noise is a dull sound that helps drown out any other noises and cheap fans actually work great because of the dull sound they make and also keep the room cool.

SLEEPING BUDDY – your child may like a security item to help them sleep. A sleeping buddy is a great way to teach your child an important skill of self-soothing. This gives them a chance to learn how to help themselves when you may not be right there to help out. Make sure your child uses this every time they sleep but, don't use this as a toy. It should only be associated with sleep or comfort! You can use another comfort item (blanket or another stuffed animal, NOT a pacifier!) during the daytime or at daycare or pre-school, if allowed.

Setting up bedtime

Setting the right bedtime for your child's age will help their body develop a natural sleep/awake rhythm (circadian rhythm). An important aspect to this is having an early bedtime, because this will allow your child to get the right amount of hours of sleep at night. Don't think that an overtired child will sleep more and longer, in fact the opposite happens!

Children up to 2.5 years old do best with a bedtime around 7:00 to 7:30 pm. Children 3.5 up to 6 years old do best with a bedtime between 7:30 to 8:30 pm.

Along with setting up the right bed time for your child's age, it's also important to have a bedtime routine. This routine should be around 30 minutes and the same every night. This helps your child's body and brain transition into night time and also make a connection that this process means sleep is soon.

An example of a night time routine looks like this:

- Bath (if giving that night)

- PJ's (pyjamas)

- Brush teeth

- One to two calm books or calm songs

- Bed

BEDTIME ROUTINE
1 Bath
2 Pyjamas
3 Teeth
4 Stories
5 Bed
6 Light's off
click
7 Goodnight!

Helping your child relax

Talk with your child about how their body feels. Ask them to feel how heavy their arms and legs feel in their bed. Can they make them feel even heavier? Have them take some slow, deep breaths to relax their body.

Read in a slow, quiet and calm way to promote sleep. You might feel silly at first reading like you are talking to them as if they were getting a massage, but this promotes a relaxation response in the body. Talk quietly and slowly, while stopping to take deep breaths throughout the book.

Do you know that it takes our bodies 10 – 15 minutes to fall to sleep and that is normal? So, it's ok if it takes your child 10 to 15 minutes after they lay down to fall asleep. This is healthy and in fact, if they fall asleep too quickly it may mean they are overtired and could possibly sleep worse at night. Allowing them to relax their bodies before falling asleep helps their overall quality of sleep, leading to a healthier child.

About the Author

Courtney Landin is a Family Health Coach focusing on exercise, nutrition, and sleep to help your family thrive in this busy world. Sleep is one of the most important aspects for a family to thrive since it regulates mood, allows kids to grow and develop, learn, and also effects weight. If you are looking to make one improvement towards a healthier life, take a look at your sleep!

Photo by: Karin Boo